How to De-stress The Mind~Body~Soul

Your Practical Guide To

De-Stressing & Therapy Journal

Victoria C. Cooper

How to De-stress The Mind ~ Body ~ Soul

How to De-stress the Mind Body Soul: Your Practical Guide to De-Stressing & Therapy Journal

ISBN-13: 978-1495423659
ISBN-10: 1495423654

Published by Light of Es'Scents by Victoria * Sanford, Florida

Book cover by: LOE Graphic Designs

Website: **www.victoriaccooper.com**

Unless otherwise indicated, all Scripture references are inspired by The Message Version of the Bible.

Dedication

I dedicate this book to each and every person who is experiencing some kind of stress in your mind, body and soul because of life's many situations,

To my beloved sons CURTIS YOUNG and CHRISTOPHER YOUNG my pride and joy,

To my mother
APOSTLE CAROLYN COOPER of
Prayer World Central International, Inc.
Who taught me how to love and have faith in GOD and the power of prayer which has taught me to de-stress in my darkest days,

And to the memory of my beloved father,
ALFRED COOPER,
Who always told me that working hard will pay off and to never let go of your dreams. He would often say, "Set a goal in life and go after it". While growing up, he always said he would retire by the age of 50 and he did it at 49!
I miss him so much. This is for you daddy!

To my brothers,
Anthony Cooper & Alonzo Arnette Cooper
Thank you for always having your baby sisters back!
To my sister,
Cynthia Cooper-Felder, for always showing me we can do anything we put our minds to
To my Brother in-law Christopher D. Felder, Thank you for believing in my dreams and being my NY promoter
To my Sister in-law Lisa Cooper, thank for your love and support.
To my nieces and nephews, love you all!

Encouragement

"Don't fret or worry. Instead of worrying, pray. Let petitions and praises shape your worries into prayers, letting God know your concerns. Before you know it, a sense of God's wholeness, everything coming together for good, will come and settle you down. It's wonderful what happens when Christ displaces worry at the center of your life.

Summing it all up, friends, I'd say you'll do best by filling your minds and meditating on things true, noble, reputable, authentic, compelling, gracious—the best, not the worst; the beautiful, not the ugly; things to praise, not things to curse. Put into practice what you learned from me, what you heard and saw and realized. Do that, and God, who makes everything work together, will work you into his most excellent harmonies."

Philippians 4: 6-9

Medical Disclaimer

Any information found in "How to De-stress the Mind, Body, and Soul" is for general, educational and informational purposes only. The information in this book is not intended or otherwise implied to be medical advice.

You should always contact your physician or health care provider to determine if this information will work for you. The information in "How to De-stress the Mind, Body, and Soul" is based on my personal experiences and is not a substitute for obtaining professional advice.

Contents

Preface..9

1~Identifying Stress..............................11

2~Effects of Stress..................................17

3~Methods to De-Stress..........................23

4~Mind Renewal &
Deleting the Negative........................33

5~Get the Body Right............................43

6~Feeding the Soul................................49

7~Write It & Visualize It.........................55

De-Stress Therapy.................................61

Contact the Author.............................75

Preface

In everyday life we all are faced with challenges that cause stress! Whether it is from work, family or health issues, seen and unforeseen pressures and tension prevents us from living a productive and peaceful life.

For me, a lot of stress comes with being a single mother of two teenage boys, working a full-time job, running a small business and trying to maintain a social life. I had to learn how to manage the anxieties and difficulties that come with balancing everyday life.

I was inspired to write this book to help others de-stress from the many responsibilities and situations in life. I wanted to encourage individuals and let them know that you can live a healthy and prosperous regardless of any circumstances that come your way.

In this book, I will share with you some tips and techniques that helped me deal with everyday life. I will show you what I learned that helped me manage stress and de-stress in order to maintain peace. I pray that you will enjoy "How to De-Stress the Mind-Body-Soul" and apply these de-stressing methods to your life.

God Bless,
Victoria

In Order to

De-Stress

You Must First

Identify Your Stress!

~ CHAPTER 1~

Identifying Stress

Stress is often assumed to be something of a bad nature. However, this is not always the case.

Everyday life situations and thoughts about those situations, can simply cause you stress.

You may be feeling overwhelmed, angry, frustrated or just drained from all energy.

Stress is the response you get when facing circumstances that force you to act, change, or adjust in some way to maintain your balance.

There's good stress and bad stress that we all have to deal with at some time of our life.

Even good stress if not handled properly can turn into bad stress. Therefore, it is vital for you to identify any life changing event in order to manage and maintain balance.

Here are a few identifiable stresses:

- Being laid off from a job.
- An argument with a spouse, boyfriend, friend or family member.
- Not having enough money to meet monthly bills.
- A child misbehaving.
- A promotion on your job that requires more responsibilities.
- A new addition to your family: such as an elderly parent or newborn baby.
- Having to find money to send your child to college.

The term "stress" refers to the response you have when facing circumstances that force you to act, change, or adjust in some way to maintain your balance!

Life comes with many responsibilities, obligations or "the wearing of many hats" which can lead to frustration, lack of patience, or just being overwhelmed. Therefore you may find yourself, sometimes, saying one or more of these phrases while trying to balance your life.

- "I need a break!"
- "These kids are driving me crazy!"
- "I feel like I'm going crazy!"
- "I just want to scream!"
- "This is too much for me to handle!"
- "There are not enough hours in the day!"
- "Why me?"
- "Help, I'm Stressed out!"
- "Please pray for me!"
- "Why did they say that?"

- "I need to get away!"
- "I can't take it anymore!"
- "I'm tired of dealing with this!"
- "I'm sick of him/her/them!"
- "I am not appreciated!"

Whether it is good stress or bad stress, stress can have a negative and an unhealthy effect. In the next chapter you will learn how stress can affect the mind, body and soul.

In Order to

De-Stress,

You Must Know the

Effects of Stress!

~ CHAPTER 2~

Effects of Stress

Stress is real and can have a detrimental effect on your mind & body and soul.

Being a single mother of two teenage sons, working a full time job, starting a business and running a household, I found myself overwhelmed with stress. Stress started affecting my thoughts, emotions and my physical well being. I had gone through a divorce and found myself stressed to the point where I felt myself wanting to shut down. Instead of dealing with my situations, I suppressed a lot of things, hoping they would just go away. There were times I just wanted to disconnect from everything and everyone and just be alone. I kept thinking to myself, "What if I have a nervous breakdown, become extremely ill or unable to function for myself?" The pressure of my situation was so extreme, that my mind kept wondering "Who is going to pick up the pieces and make sure life continues for me and my sons?"

When stress hits, sometimes you will not know the magnitude of its effects until you notice the negative impact of your day obligations or until it's too late. I personally did not understand how stress was affecting my mind, body and soul while I was trying to deal with all of my issues. Issues such as, not having enough money to cover expenses, raising two boys as a single mom, relationship issues and list goes on. I did not know that not wanting to deal with anyone or anything, being confused, hurt, scared, exhausted, sick, and in pain all the time was due to the stress that was in my life.

It's scary to think, that according to www.apa.org, 43% of individuals suffer health effects from stress. Also, 70% of visits to a doctor are stress related complaints.

If stress is not managed properly, it can disrupt your sense of well-being, leave you feeling overwhelmed, helpless and lead to unwarranted illnesses.

Here are a few of areas that stress can have a negative effect in your mind, body and emotions:

- **Hair**: High Stress levels may cause excessive hair loss and some baldness.
- **Muscles**: Spasms pain in the neck and shoulders, musculoskeletal aches, lower back pain and various minor muscular twitches often appear from stress.
- **Digestive tract**: Stress can cause aggravate disease of the digestive track including gastritis, stomach ulcers and irritable colon.
- **Skin**: Some individuals react to stress with outbreak of skin problems such as eczema and psoriasis.
- **Brain**: Stress triggers mental and emotional problems such as insomnia, headaches, personality changes, irritability anxiety and depression.
- **Mouth**: Mouth ulcers and excessive dryness are often signs of stress.
- **Heart**: Cardio vascular disease and hypertension are linked to accumulated stress.
- **Lungs**: High level of mental or emotional stress

affects individuals with asthmatic conditions.

- **Reproductive organs**: Stress affects the reproductive system causing menstrual disorders and recurrent vaginal infections in women and impotence and premature ejaculation in men.

There are several areas in life that can cause stress. Here is a list of arming percentages of stressful situations individuals deal with on a daily basis.

- Money issues (69 %)
- Work related issues (65 %)
- The economy (61 %)
- Family responsibilities (57 %)
- Relationships (56 %)
- Family health problems (52 %)

Believe or not, stress plays a big part in our physical illness as well as mental or emotional problems!

Once we identify stress and know the effects it causes, then it's possible to move forward and learn how to de-stress in order to live a healthy and a productive life. It's important to know some tools and methods to use when life's responsibilities start to get too much for you to handle.

In the next chapter, I will cover practical ways to help you de-stress.

In Order to

De-Stress,

You Must Know the

Methods to

De-Stress!

~ CHAPTER 3 ~

Methods to De-stress

Stress is inevitable and you will need to learn what to do to manage your life when it occurs. You will have to look for the signs of stress and if you feel it's overtaking you, start seeking help immediately!

In this chapter, I will go over some practical methods you can do to help you de-stress your mind, body and soul.

For the past two decades, I had to learn multiple ways to help me get through some really stressful situations. I had to come to grips with myself, stop, look my situations head on and say, "WAIT! I NEED TO TAKE SOME TIME FOR MYSELF!" During those times, I used simple creative methods to help me alleviate stress until I could deal with my situations.

These techniques will allow you to think clearer, live better and be able to deal with stressful situations when they arise.

RELAXATION

The best way for you to immediately get relief from stress is to simply, ***relax***! It is important for you to become less anxious and less tense as soon as possible. Make it a point to block out time in your daily schedule to make sure you take the time to relax. You can start out with just 30 minutes a day. When you take time to relax, you will immediately start to de-stress, which will allow you to think clearly and move forward with calmness.

DOWNTIME

Allowing you to have moments of quality "downtime" can give immediate relaxation as well. It's imperative that you "steal away" and find some downtime in order to relax from any and all stressful situations.

What happens during DOWNTIME?

- You are usually or sometimes alone
- You are in silence; quiet, no noise
- You do not have children around
- You can gather your thoughts
- You can relax your mind
- You can meditate and reflect
- You can regroup, gain perspective and focus
- You can rejuvenate your mind, body and soul
- You are still; sometimes no activity or movement
- You are able to think & plan

Relaxation keeps stress from building up and helps you to de-stress!

AROMATHERAPY

In 2009, I started my luxury soy candle business, Light of Es'Scents by Victoria. Candles have been a great stress reliever for me with their aromatherapy benefits. It was through my most stressful times of my life that I utilized aromatherapy for relief. When you use candles, the low light that comes from the actual candle is captured by your sight and sent straight to your brain. Even today, aromatherapy is a popular and constant method people use to de-stress. Using aromatherapy a few minutes a day will allow your body to relax. You will feel yourself start to unwind, feel less tense and feel emotionally and physically better.

Aromatherapy is often used as an alternative approach for helping the mind, body and soul relax. The use of fragrances creates an atmosphere that stimulates the senses. Science and research has shown that many moods and negative emotions can be lifted just by a fragrance or scent.

You can start by taking 30 minutes to yourself, run a nice warm bath, with soft music playing in the background, turn the lights down or off, with only the candles as your light, and melt away the stress. The warm water will also relax your tense muscles and as an option, adding bubbles or bath salts will add additional aromatherapy.

Another way to relax is to use candles while you read a book, magazine or doing paperwork in order to enjoy the relaxing benefits of aromatherapy.

Life can be tough therefore stress is evitable.

Thankfully, aromatherapy and candles can help relieve some of the stress! Start today, take some well deserve time for yourself and try some of these tips to help eliminate the stress in your life. You can visit my website **www.loebyvictoria.com**, get a candle today and start relaxing.

A few great aromatherapy scents:

Lavender- soothing and relaxing; said to help relieve stress, depression, anxiety, and nervous disorders; used to treat headaches and to have less difficulty falling asleep; some find it useful during childbirth; nice in bedroom and bath.

Citrus scents- grapefruit, lemon, orange, etc… invigorating and brightens the mood of a room; uplifting and clean; eliminates anxiety and stress; in a study of lemon scents it caused the biggest drop in mistakes during keyboard typing; helps you concentrate.

Vanilla- sweet scent known to be a natural aphrodisiac; naturally warming and soothing; relaxing and comforting; thoughts of favorite foods and happy memories of home and childhood.

Cinnamon- helps with exhaustion and fatigue; wonderful effects on nerves; calms you down and makes you more aware.

Sandalwood- relaxing and calming ability; helps soothe irritation and lifts depression; associated with meditation.

Eucalyptus Spearmint-relaxing and great for mental mind clearing.

PRACTICE BREATHING TECHNIQUES

Taking a deep breath is one of the best ways to reduce stress. Slow down and actively concentrate on your breathing. Start off inhaling deeply as you count to five, hold your breath for five seconds, then exhale slowly, counting to five. Do this ten to fifteen times to relax your nerves and muscles. As you breathe out, visualize the stress leaving your body though your breath. Taking the time to make deep breathing part of your daily routine will immediately allow your mind, body and soul to de-stress.

TURN OFF YOUR PHONE

When you are trying to de-stress you should eliminate all distractions! Sometimes the pressure of constantly answering emails, taking phone calls or checking for voice mails can become overwhelming. Research says smart phones are linked to increased stress in a person's life. Try turning off your phone and television for about one hour. The thought of not having the urge to pick up your cell can bring immediately relaxation. Turning off your phone might be a little hard for you in the beginning, but it will work! It will help you completely relax and refocus.

PLAN A DAY FOR YOU

Doing something out of your normal routine yields excitement, happiness and will allow you to de-stress. Whether driving to the beach or going to the movies, take the time and plan to do something just for you. Changing your surrounding can make you feel like you're on a mini vacation. You can start by getting a massage at your local spas but most important thing is to do something you enjoy.

GET PLENTY OF SLEEP

Sleep is the first thing that is sacrificed when you are stressed or overwhelmed. However, one of the biggest health mistakes you can make with your health is not getting enough sleep. Getting adequate sleep allows your body to recharge and to become refreshed. Getting proper sleep allows your body to rid itself of excess hormones and built up toxins that cause a never ending cycle of stress. Start today and try to get 7-9 hours of sleep on a nightly basis.

LAUGH AND SMILE

Laughter is said to be the best medicine! Whether renting, buying or going to see a funny movie, laughter is guaranteed to help eliminate stress. Research tells us those smiling and laughing releases endorphins, which fights stress, helps to relax and reminds you that life is more than just work. Even if it feels strange at first, make it a point to smile more often.

"A happy heart is good medicine and a cheerful mind works healing, but a broken spirit dries up the bones."
Proverbs 17:22 (AMP)

Since stress can come in different forms, it imperative to take time to regroup and refocus on a daily basis. It is very important for your overall being, to be able to balance yourself by taking some well needed time for you.

Remember stress is inevitable and having methods to de-stress is important. Using these methods does not mean you will not have any more stress, but it will help bring some relief during your present stressful situation.

Using some of these methods will allow you a little time, hopefully, to figure out what you can do differently to get better results the next time you are faced with difficulty, pressure or tension.

Don't worry, in the next chapter, I will show you where to begin your journey of balance. I will show you, not only where to start but also how to have a defense against the negative effects of stress.

In Order to De-Stress, You Must Renew Your Mind & Delete the Negative!

~ CHAPTER 4~

Mind Renewal & Deleting the Negative

'Summing it all up, friends, I'd say you'll do best by filling your minds and meditating on things true, noble, reputable, authentic, compelling, gracious – the best, not the worst; the beautiful, not the ugly; things to praise, not things to curse. Put into practice what you learned from me, what you heard and saw and realized. Do that, and God, who makes everything work together, will work you into his most excellent harmonies!"
Philippians 4:8-9

Every single thing begins with a thought!

Your **mind** is the element that enables you to be aware of your experiences - how you think, feel, and view the world around you, and yet it can be your worst enemy.

As it pertains to stress, it is important to be aware of what you choose to hear, read, watch or look at in order for you to maintain peace and accomplish your dreams.

"Do not be conformed to this world, but be transformed by the renewal of your mind, that by testing you may discern what is the will of God, what is good and acceptable and perfect."
Romans 12:2 (ESV)

A prerequisite to renewing your mind is to be alone in order to clear and rid your mind of any and all negative thoughts. This will allow you to start refocusing and start thinking specifically on positive things.

Each day, I have a daily routine while driving to work. I try not listening to the radio or CD every morning. I make a conscious choice to drive in silence. Silence allows me the time to pray and seek God for the answers I need in order to deal with my stressful situations. For me, silence starts the process of renewing my mind. Silence allows my mind, emotions and spirit to become centered and grounded in order to have peace at the beginning of my day. If you make a conscious effort to just try it, you will begin to see it really works. Having quiet time with God, first, is essential to renewing your mind. It sets the tone for the day for what lies ahead.

> *"First and foremost, you have to take time to quiet your mind on a daily basis"*

Negativity be Gone!

Negativity can come in different forms. It can come from negativity from within, in relationships or from our everyday surroundings.

Once you get to your destination and throughout the day and every day, continue to renew your mind by guarding it with what you hear.

Self

Have you ever had a great idea and talked yourself out if it? Do you constantly find yourself saying, "I can never do that? Or "This will never work"?

Negative thinking brings anxiety and can cause stress in your life. You have to immediately renew your mind by counter attacking negative speaking by declaring positive sayings like "That's a great idea!", "I can do that!" or "It will work!" Start releasing the fear of "What if" and replace it with "I can!"

"I can do all things through Christ who strengthens me"
Philippians 4:13 (NKJ)

Start today to focus on things that you want to do in life and see yourself achieving each and every one of those goals.

People

Have you ever been around negative talking people and after having a conversation with them you feel worse or have a headache after listening to them? Have you ever had a close friend or relative tell you that something will never work, your idea is crazy or no one has ever done that before? When times were tough because of some bad decisions that you made, did you hear people say, you will never come out of that trouble, or your situation is just too bad to correct? Or have you ever had a close friend or relative continue to bring up your stressful situations without offering solutions? Well, from this point on, stop listening to negative people!

If your mind continues to dwell on the words that people around you say, you will never de-stress or have faith to achieve your dreams! For me, I had to make a clear distinction of who was in my corner and who was not in my corner very quickly. I had to discern who wanted me to be stress free and who was adding stress to my life, which leads me to relationships.

Relationships

Have you ever been in a relationship where someone made you feel bad about yourself? Try to tear you down? Make you feel less than a person? Make you feel not smart enough? Talk unkind words to you that hurt you to the core?

Unhealthy relationship will cause stress and will yield negative effects on your mind, body and soul.

For years, I suffered and endured issues of abuse within my marriage. I knew I was in an unhealthy marriage but I was worried about what people were going to say and think. I really struggled with people's opinion of my situation or me. I didn't want to hear the "I told you so", or "wow, her marriage didn't last! Abusive or toxic relationships are not just physical, but also mental and verbal.

Most times, we know when we are in toxic and abusive relationships. I believe that pride, pleasing people and fear of the unknown keeps us from choosing to make a conscious decision for our own life's sake.

If you don't break the cycle now, you will keep going through the same thing, getting the same results. And if you have children, they can grow up possibly, thinking abuse is an acceptable and appropriate behavior.

You can't live your life for other people or through other people. You have to do what's best for you and your children. You don't have to be ashamed! Hold your head up and be proud of yourself! You deserve to be treated with love and respect.

Start today making better choices for your life! Surround yourself with people who speak positive and productive things. Surround yourself with people who are going to celebrate you and encourage you to continue to have balance and a stress-free life. You will be amazed how your mind will start to transform by the power of words and always remember your worth.

"Words kill, words give life;
they're either poison or fruit – you choose."
Proverbs 18:21

Surroundings

A major key to disengaging negativity is to do what

you love. We all have to make a living in order to sustain ourselves and our families. When you do what you love it allows you to feel at peace and good about yourself.

If you are fortunate to have a job you love, remember these key facts so that you can always delete any negative thoughts and keep your mind renewed.

- Atmosphere is everything! Be conscious to protect the area where you work and live with peace and tranquility as much as possible. Whether it's soft music or the Word of God, visual affirmations on your desk, wall or notebook, will assure your mind is renewed each and every day. Remember, negative people sometimes hate positive, happy and focused people. Their bitterness and unfortunate problems can cause you to be burden and overwhelmed. So keeping motivational and inspirational messages within reach is a must to help you stay aligned with your goals and dreams.

On the other hand, if you are not fortunate, at the moment, to have a job you love, remember these key facts, in order to delete any negative thoughts and to keep your mind renewed.

- Make a list of your dreams and goals and revisit them on daily basis. Renewing your mind with your dreams will motivate and encourage you on your journey.

- Be proud of yourself no matter where you work, for now. Remember, you are actively and responsibly doing something to sustain you and your family and that is honorable.

" For even when we were with you, this we commanded you, that if any would not work, neither should he eat."
II Thessalonians 3:10 (KJV)

Remember everything begins to de-stress when you renew your mind! Once you start the process of mind renewal, you will begin to de-stress, maintain balance in your life and begin to manage any seen and unforeseen pressures.

In the next chapter I will teach you another important step to de-stressing, the importance of maintaining a healthy body.

In Order to

De-Stress,

You Must Get the

Body Right!

~ CHAPTER 5~

Get the Body Right

Your body is your most important asset! It is vital that you take care of it daily in order to live a healthy life.

By the grace of God, I have lived to reach my forties! And I can proudly and thankfully say this is the best I have ever felt in my life! Over the past 15 years, stressful situations took a great toll on my mind and my body. I often hear countless stories of people in their forties who have had strokes and even ultimately dying. After surviving painful situations and experiences in my mind and body, I made a promise to myself that I would take better care of my mental, emotional and physical health.

God made you exactly how you are in order for you to do your part and maintain what He has created in you.

"...How truly I love you! We're the best of friends, and I pray for good fortune in everything you do, and for your good health – that your everyday affairs prosper, as well as your soul!"
3 John 1:2

Knowing how to de-stress your body, is very important for your overall life and health. Stress is said to be the root cause of a lot of heart disease, diabetes and strokes.

Exercise

Exercise drastically reduces stress! When you work out aerobically or doing cardio, it releases endorphins and adrenaline, which is the body's natural "feel-good" hormone.

Exercise will increase your overall health and your sense of well-being. Virtually any form of exercise, from aerobics, walking, swimming, biking or weight training, can act as a stress reliever.

Regular exercise can increase your self-confidence and lower the symptoms associated with mild depression and anxiety. It actually will improve your mood and help to improve your sleep, which is greatly disrupted by stress. All this can ease your stress levels and give you a sense of command over your body and your life.

Any form of physical activity can help you unwind and become an important part of your de-stressing process. A little exercise can go a long way towards eliminating stress even if you have not worked out in a long time. However, if you haven't exercised for some time and you have health concerns, please consult a doctor before starting a new exercise routine.

Any form of physical activity can help you relax, unwind and become an important part of your de-stressing process!

Working out with a friend, co-worker or family member often brings a new level of motivation and commitment to your workouts as well.

It's all about getting started. A 20-minute walk or jog around your block can yield up to 12 hours of improved mood and make a big difference in reducing stress levels.

Eating

What you eat makes a difference in your mind and body while de-stressing. Eating well can help your mind and body feel balanced and healthy, making you less susceptible to spikes in blood sugar and feelings of anxiety.

A few things that you can start doing to de-stress are to avoid eating refined sugar found in certain foods. Carbohydrates, such as pasta, convert easily to sugar. These can cause severe ups and downs in your blood sugar and lead to agitation; upsetting your body's ability to efficiently utilize energy.

Another thing you can do to de-stress is to avoid excessive caffeine. Having too much caffeine can make you jumpy and irritable. Start today keeping your morning intake of caffeine moderate and steady every day. Also, try not to drink caffeine after 1 or 2 in the afternoon. If you must have more coffee than you should, switch to decaf or an herbal tea with little or no caffeine.

When you eat fresh fruits, vegetables and whole grains that are free of refined sugar you won't be tired and groggy, but energized and focused. Replacing refined sugar with foods like apples, grapes, carrots, broccoli, brown rice or whole grain breads will allow you to maintain good health.

When you start eating plenty of low-calorie protein, such as chicken, fish, whole grains, dark leafy vegetables or low-fat dairy, they will give you a better source of energy.

Supplements

Supplements simply enhance your overall health for the better. When you take a multi-vitamin, you are giving your body the necessary essentials that can relieve stress. Taking Vitamin B and Vitamin D are especially good for relaxation.

Remember, your body is your most important asset! Start today to do your part to maintain what God created. Eat fresh fruits, vegetables, whole grains, and protein and drink lots of water. Getting your body right and being conscious of your overall health will reduce a tremendous amount of pressure and tension in your life.

In the next chapter, we will focus on how feeding your soul is vital in eliminating stress.

In Order to De-Stress, You Must Feed the Soul!

~ CHAPTER 6~

Feeding the Soul

The Word of God and the Power of Prayer are two great forms of stress relief!

"...How truly I love you! We're the best of friends, and I pray for good fortune in everything you do, and for your good health – that your everyday affairs prosper, as well as your soul!"
3 John 1:2

It is the will of God for you to be in good health as well as believe on His son Jesus Christ. God knew the cares of this world would be overwhelming at times, and gave you two powerful tools to use to help you de-stress your mind, body and soul.

"Because if you acknowledge and confess with your lips that Jesus is Lord and in your heart believe (adhere to, trust in, and rely on the truth) that God raised Him from the dead, you will be saved."
Romans 10:9 (AMP)

The knowledge of having faith in God, believing He knows what is best for you and most importantly that He will look after you. By praying to God for help, especially during stressful times, you can rest assured that God is listening to you and He cares.

"Casting the whole of ***your*** *care [all* ***your*** *anxieties, all* ***your*** *worries, all* ***your*** *concerns, once and for all] on Him, for He* ***cares*** *for you affectionately and* ***cares*** *about you watchfully."*
I Peter 5:7

Dealing with life can be stressful all by itself. There are times you don't literally know what to do, don't have anyone to talk to and just feel all alone. If you have issues that are causing stress in your marriage, health, children and finances, it can be even more overwhelming.

I have seen and experience many times like those in my life. The only solution that helped me de-stress from my problems was my relationship with God. I am so grateful to my mother Apostle Carolyn Cooper, who taught me how to pray. Prayer is and can be a vital part of feeding your soul and eliminating stress!

No matter how hopeless your situation may be, have faith, miracles do happen!

"And Jesus looking upon them saith, With men it is impossible, but not with God: for with God all things are possible."

Mark 10:27 (KJV)

Prayer

Start today and incorporate a regular prayer schedule into your life. It doesn't take much time or effort to say a small prayer when you wake up and/or before you go to bed. It is your opportunity to thank God for His continual blessings. The more you do this, the more blessings you will receive. Over time, you will find that your life will become easier, and hence less stressful. And if times get tough, your strengthened spirit will help you deal with stress better.

The Word of God

Start today to incorporate a regular Bible reading schedule into your life as well! Whether you start with one verse a day, feeding your soul with the Word of God will not only de-stress you, but give you wisdom knowledge and understanding in any area of your life!

"For the Word that God speaks is alive and full of power [making it active, operative, energizing, and effective]; it is sharper than any two-edged sword, penetrating to the dividing line of the breath of life (soul) and [the immortal] spirit, and of joints and marrow [of the deepest parts of our nature], exposing *and* sifting *and* analyzing *and* judging the very thoughts and purposes of the heart"
Hebrews 4:12 (AMP)

The use of prayer is a great form of stress relief!

Here are 6 encouraging scriptures that I confessed with my mouth on a daily basis when stress took control of my mind and body. Start today confessing these scriptures out loud on your de-stressing journey. As you confess, have faith and believe! God will give you the peace and answers your need for everything that concerns you.

1. Proverbs 3:5-12 ~ "Trust GOD from the bottom of your heart; don't try to figure out everything on your own. Listen for GOD's voice in everything you do, everywhere you go; he's the one who will keep you on track"

2. Proverbs 16:3 ~ "Put GOD in charge of your work, then what you've planned will take place"

3. Psalm 34:17-19 ~ "Is anyone crying for help? GOD is listening, ready to rescue you. If your heart is broken, you'll find GOD right there; if you're kicked in the gut, he'll help you catch your breath. Disciples so often get into trouble; still, GOD is there every time"

4. Matthew 11:28-30 (AMP) ~ "Come to Me, all you who labor and are heavy-laden and overburdened and I will cause you to rest. [I will ease and relieve and refresh your souls.] Take My yoke upon you and learn of Me, for I am gentle (meek) and humble (lowly) in heart, and you will find rest (relief and ease and refreshment and recreation and blessed quiet) for your souls. For My yoke is wholesome (useful, good—not harsh, hard, sharp, or pressing, but comfortable, gracious, and pleasant), and My burden is light and easy to be borne"

5. Romans 8:28 (AMP) ~ "We are assured and know that God being a partner in their labor, all things work together and are befitting into a plan for good to and for those who love God and are called according to His design and purpose"

6. Proverbs 16:3 (~ "Commit to the Lord whatever you do, and your plans will succeed"

In Order to

De-Stress,

It's Important to
Write & Visualize!

~ CHAPTER 7~

Write it & Visual it

KEEP A JOURNAL

Writing is another powerful tool to use to de-stress! All it takes is a few minutes a day to unload your mind and revisit your dreams!

Doing this task is an automatic de-stressor. In addition to de-stressing, it motivates, encourages and keeps you moving forward with your dreams or daily tasks.

You can pick up a very inexpensive notebook and pen from any store. Start writing and charting a new strategy towards getting back your peace and maintaining a solid de-stressing plan. Writing and

Visualizing will allow you to start a new course in life or revisit the old dreams that you have not completed.

> *Writing down your thoughts can be therapeutic! Taking the time to write what you honestly feel on the inside about your situation is a great de-stressing technique!*

"And then GOD answered: "'Write this.
Write what you see.
Write it out in big block letters
so that it can be read on the run.
This vision-message is a witness
pointing to what's coming.
It aches for the coming – it can hardly wait!
And it doesn't lie.
If it seems slow in coming, wait.
It's on its way. It will come right on time." Habakkuk 2

At the very moment you start feeling stressed, it is very important to identify that stress. Write down what's causing the stress and then what de-stress method you can used alleviate that stress.

Next, to get you started on your journey to de-stress your mind, body and soul, I have provided for you a de-stress therapy journal.

It is a self-assessment exercise designed to help you:

- Identify all stresses in your life
- Identify all effects these stresses are having in your mind, body and soul (And the de-stressing methods you will return your peaceful balance)
- Identify and plan to feed your soul, delete the negative and be proactive with your surroundings
- Identify healthy options for your body
- Revisit your dreams and create and action plan to fulfilled each one

Your De-Stress Therapy Self-Assessment exercise will allow you to pin point, truthfully, once and for all, what is causing stress in your life. It will also start you on your journey to becoming stress free and live your life to the fullest!

Remember words give life! After you have completed your De-stress Therapy Assignment, I have provided a list of declarations for you to confess, out loud, each and every day. These declarations will build faith in your spirit. They will become the power you need on your journey to de-stressing your mind, body and soul!

"Words kill, words give life;
they're either poison or fruit – you choose"
Proverbs 18:21

God did it for me and God will do it for you!

I'm praying for you & with you!

From my heart to yours,

Victoria

My Understanding of My Truth & Reality In Order to De-Stress My Life

De-Stress Therapy

Self-Assessment Assignment

Life is not easy! Stress is real and stress happens to all of us! However stress can be managed! My stressful experiences affected my mind, body and soul. Thankfully, through prayer and my love and faith in God, I found the help I needed to de-stress.

"And Peter opened his mouth and said: Most certainly and thoroughly I now perceive and understand that God shows no partiality and is no respecter of persons" Acts 10:34 (AMP)

Before you start your self-assessment assignment, try some of the de-stressing methods listed in Chapter 3. De-stressing before this exercise will allow your mind and body to relax. Next, pray and read a scripture. Prayer and the Word of God are two great de-stressing methods to eliminate any kind of stress! Your mind and emotions will become calmer after prayer and your spirit will be at ease when you feed it with the Word of God!

"Ask, and it shall be given you; seek, and ye shall find; knock and it shall be opened unto you: For every one that asketh receiveth;

and he that seeketh findeth; and to him that knocketh it shall be opened" Matthew 7:7-8 (KJV)

As you read and answer each self-assessment statement, do so thoughtfully. Search your inner being and be truthful. Remember, in order to eliminate the effects of stress, you must identify stress.

Once you have completed your De-Stress Therapy, start affirming a peaceful mind, body and soul by speaking with encouraging words every day. I have provided a List of Declarations that will help you, de-stress your life! Words are powerful! And Words can give life!

"Words kill, words give life;
they're either poison or fruit – you choose" Proverbs 18:21

You are now on your way to beginning a new stress-free managed life! Relax and don't be anxious! Life is a journey, so remember to take it one day at a time.

It's Time to Live Life to the Fullest!

Your De-Stressing Journey Starts Now!

My Personal Journal

These are the things that give me stress:

These are the things that are happening in my life as a result of those stresses:

<u>These are the things I will start doing daily in order to eliminate the stress in my life</u>:

These are the things I will start doing daily to renew my mind in order to transform my thinking and delete negative thoughts:

These are the things I will start doing daily in order to become healthy:

These are the necessary things that I will start doing daily in order to feed my soul:

These are the things that will make my life peaceful & enjoyable:

These are the things I will start doing daily in order to make those peaceful and enjoyable things happen:

"My Mind, Body & Soul are Becoming Stress Free Every day!"

Read the declaration out loud on the next page and sign your name. By doing this you will be making a commitment to yourself that you will take the necessary step to de-stress your Mind, Body and Soul and start your de-stressing journey to a new you!

DECLARATIONS!

- I will immediately identify any stress!
- I will immediately recognize the effects of any stress!
- I will immediately start to use methods to de-stress!
- I will daily renew my mind & delete all negative thoughts!
- I will daily put forth effort to keep my body healthy!
- I will daily feed my soul with the word of God and positive affirmations!
- I will write, consistently visualize and daily work to make my dreams come true!
- I am living a stress free life!

X______________________________

References

American Institute of Stress
http://www.stress.org/

American Psychological Association
Press Release-Stress in America, Impact of Stress
http://www.apa.org

Klinic Community Health
http://www.de-stress.ca/

Contact the Author

Please feel free to visit our website or email the author to hold a De-Stressing class or host a Light of Es'Scents Luxury Soy Candle Party.

Victoria is available for speaking engagements, workshops, conferences or book club signing and presentations.

Please contact at:

~

Victoria C. Cooper

Sanford, Florida 32771

Visit website below:

www.victoriaccooper.com

Email: **loebyvictoria@gmail.com**

Made in the USA
Charleston, SC
18 April 2014